VICTORIAN CITY

FRANK WORSDALL

REMOVE NOT THE ANCIENT LANDMARK,
WHICH THY FATHERS HAVE SET.
Proverbs ch 22 verse 28

RICHARD DREW PUBLISHING
GLASGOW

First published 1982 by Richard Drew Publishing Ltd

This edition first published 1988 by
Richard Drew Publishing Ltd
6 Clairmont Gardens
Glasgow G3 7LW
Scotland

British Library Cataloguing in Publication Data

Worsdall, Frank
Victorian city : a selection of Glasgow's
architecture.—2nd ed.
1. Scotland. Strathclyde Region. Glasgow.
Buildings. Architectural features, 1837-1901
I. Title
720′.9414′43

ISBN 0-86267-122-1

Photographs by the author

Front cover
Templeton's Carpet Factory, Glasgow Green

Back cover
Doorway, Savings Bank   752, Argyle Street
Salmon & Gillespie   architects
Albert H Hodge   sculptor

Designed by James W Murray
Set in Ehrhardt by Swains (Glasgow) Limited
Made and Printed in Great Britain by
Butler & Tanner Ltd., Frome, Somerset

CONTENTS

CHURCHES   1

Caledonia Road U P Church   2

Trinity House   3

'The Follies'   4

'John Street Jam'   5

Lansdowne Church   6

Camphill Queen's Park Church   7

Adelaide Place Baptist Church   8

Finnieston Free Church   9

Kelvinside Hillhead Parish Church   10   11

Cathedral Square U P Church   12

Shawlands Old Parish Church   13

Saint George's in the Fields Parish Church   14

Saint Albert's Catholic Church   15

Langside Free Church   16

Queen's Cross Church   17

Kelvin Stevenson Memorial Church   18

EDUCATION   19

Dundasvale Teachers' Centre   20

Strathclyde House   21

Saint Andrew's Catholic School   22

Langside College Annexe   23   24

The University of Glasgow   25

Rockvilla School   26

Overnewton School   27

Kelvinside Academy   28   29

Bellahouston Academy   30

Abbotsford Primary School   31

Dennistoun Primary School   32

Govanhill Primary School   33

Glasgow School of Art   34   35   36

COMMERCIAL   37

Langside Hall   38

The Royal Bank of Scotland   39

36, Jamaica Street   40

70-80, Gordon Street   41

42, Virginia Street   42

The Merchants' House   43

The Stock Exchange   44

The Clydesdale Bank   45

James Sellars House   46

24, Saint Vincent Place   47

121, West George Street   48

60, Mitchell Street   49

The Savoy Centre   50

Trustee Savings Bank   51

The Clydesdale Bank   52

144, Saint Vincent Street   53

116, Hope Street   54

PUBLIC   55

147, Buchanan Street   56

40-50, Wilson Street   57

The Procurators' Library   58   59   60

109-115, Trongate   61

First Church of Christ Scientist   62   63

The Briggait Centre   64

Mitchell Library Extension   65

The Kibble Palace   66

Western Baths   67

19, McAlpine Street   68

The City Hall   69

The Victoria Infirmary   70

Pollokshields Burgh Hall   71

Govan Burgh Hall   72

DOMESTIC   73

Clarendon Place   74

Peel Terrace   75

Claremont Terrace   76

Kirklee Terrace   77

Saint Vincent Crescent   78

Grosvenor Terrace   79

25, Mansionhouse Road   80

Park Terrace   81

Park area map   82   83

Walmer Crescent   84

Broadcasting House   85

998, Great Western Road   86

Charing Cross Mansions   87

733-745, Terregles Avenue   88

Stoneleigh   89

Sunlight Cottages   90

MISCELLANEOUS   91

Wellington Memorial   92

44-54, James Watt Street   93

The Necropolis   94

The Monteath Mausoleum   94

John Henry Alexander Monument   95

Charles Tennant of Saint Rollox Monument   96

The Aiken of Dalmoak Mausoleum   97

Southern Necropolis Lodge   98

Saint Andrew's Suspension Bridge   99

60, Boden Street   100

42, Bain Street   101

Queen Street Station   102

Templeton's Business Centre   103

Sundial   The King's Park   104

The Doulton Fountain   105

Govan Shipbuilders Offices   106

Prince's Dock Pumping Station   107

The Travel Centre   108

INDEX   109

INTRODUCTION

Architecture is perhaps the most undervalued of the fine arts. The fact that its aesthetic qualities are often inextricably linked with a functional purpose makes evaluation a controversial business. One person may see a building as a masterpiece while another sees it merely as an expendable mass of stone and lime.

Mediaeval Glasgow was a small cathedral and university city which did not begin to expand until the 17th century when foreign trade became profitable on the west coast of Scotland. The agrarian and industrial revolutions had a marked effect on the city which naturally became the mercantile centre of the west. It was in the midst of the industrial upheaval that Victoria came to the throne, and for the following 64 years reigned over an increasingly prosperous nation. Glasgow was to benefit more than most from this period of affluence.

In 1837 much of the old city remained intact — the High Street, Gallowgate, Trongate, Bridgegate, Saltmarket and Stockwell — with their wynds and vennels. Georgian suburbs had spread westward over Blythswood Hill and Garnethill, as well as southwards across the river into Tradeston, Hutcheson-town and Laurieston. These were residential areas, but others like Anderston, the Calton, and Port Dundas became important industrial centres. Cotton spinning and weaving, chemical manufacture, brewing and distilling, glass and pottery making, could all be found there. The great ironfounding, engineering, ship and locomotive building works were about to start.

By the 1870s the name of Glasgow was world-famous as a centre of heavy industry and it had expanded into the second city of the Empire. The population had grown from 255,650 in 1841, to 477,732 in 1871, and by 1901 had reached 761,709.

When Queen Victoria died in 1901 Glasgow stretched from Maryhill in the north to Shawlands in the south, and from Anniesland to Parkhead. Vast new suburbs had grown up — Hillhead, Kelvinside, Hyndland, Pollokshields, Langside, Mount Florida, Govanhill, Dalmarnock and Dennistoun, to name only the most important. Some of them flouted the central authority by setting up as self-governing Police Burghs, but most of these were short-lived. Industry and commerce, despite set-backs like the bank crashes of 1857 and 1878, had reached a peak of prosperity and, despite the universal sadness felt at the old queen's death, the city looked forward to the future with supreme self-confidence.

It was confidence which inspired the builders of the Victorian city, and by the greatest good fortune they were served by a group of architects of quite exceptional merit. It is their combined efforts which make Glasgow one of the world's finest 19th century cities, and annually more and more tourists come to marvel at their achievement.

The author has chosen 100 or so of his favourite Victorian buildings in the hope of introducing them to a wider and ever more discerning public, and to encourage the more adventurous to extend their knowledge and appreciation of our priceless architectural heritage.

CHURCHES

DOORWAY
FORMER STRATHBUNGO PARISH CHURCH
601, POLLOKSHAWS ROAD

W G ROWAN ARCHITECT
1888

CALEDONIA ROAD U P CHURCH

1, Caledonia Road

Most of 'Greek' Thomson's mature buildings are in Glasgow, and one is bound to say that they have not been appreciated as they deserve. Even renovation work when undertaken seems to be half-hearted and unenthusiastic. The adulation now afforded to Mackintosh is not extended to his great predecessor.

Caledonia Road was his first and favourite church and it embodied a number of clever and original ideas which, with its superb internal decoration, were lost in the disastrous fire of 1965. It is now proposed to rehabilitate this magnificent shell as a club and restaurant.

Probably the best-known and most exciting skyline in Glasgow is that of the Park area with its four towers soaring dramatically above the roofs of the surrounding terraces. The tallest tower is that of the Free Church College and the two smaller ones in similar style belonged to the Free College Church. These two adjoining buildings were built at the same time, in 1855–1857, to the designs of Charles Wilson, and form one of his most impressive achievements.

The church was destroyed by fire in 1903 and reconstructed as the college library. The whole complex has now again been reconstructed as housing.

TRINITY HOUSE
31, Lynedoch Street

3

'THE FOLLIES'
195, Pitt Street

Another version of the Acropolis. The main front of the Erechtheion as interpreted by John Burnet for what was originally Elgin Place Congregational Church. It was opened on 3 August 1856. Impressive if not as subtle as 'Greek' Thomson would have made it.

The church closed in 1962 and its future looked bleak until its reconstruction as a restaurant and disco, in 1982.

One of many redundant city churches, but a particularly fine and interesting one. A progressive congregation, they replaced their plain old meeting-house with something calculated to impress. The architect, J T Rochead chose Italian Baroque as his style. Externally this is expressed by the massive Ionic colonnade which lit the church on the upper floor. To allow maximum light the windows are fitted directly into the stonework — a bold and uncommon feature.

The design reached its climax with a magnificent, elaborate plaster ceiling. After thirty years of disuse the building has been converted into a restaurant.

'JOHN STREET JAM'

18, John Street

LANSDOWNE CHURCH

420, Great Western Road

This outstanding Early English Gothic church with its slender 218 ft spire is a conspicuous landmark in the north-west of the city. It established John Honeyman, its architect, as one of the foremost in the city. An authority on medieval churches, at Lansdowne he provided a building which married an academic approach to architecture with the latest requirements. It illustrates the Tractarian influence which was beginning to make itself felt in Scotland in the 1860s. There are transepts and an apse, but still the Presbyterian gallery around three sides.

Sculpture plays an important part in the design. William Mossman carved the medallions flanking the elaborate porch, but all the rest is by James Shanks. Stained glass formed part of the original scheme, designed by Hughes of London, but it pales into insignificance beside Alfred Webster's two magnificent transept windows of 1914.

William Leiper's architectural horizon was considerably widened by a sojourn in London where the Gothic style had become a religious and architectural cult. Camphill U P Church is the second of his four Glasgow churches and is arguably the finest. Said to have been inspired by an example in Caen in Normandy, it was opened in October 1876 with the spire still unbuilt. Luckily, this fine feature was completed in 1883.

The design is massive and bold in outline, softened with sculpture sensitively placed. John Mossman carved the angel with outstretched wings on the front.

The interior is equally impressive. The wide nave is flanked by aisles and transepts which contain the galleries. The decoration included elaborate stencilled ornament on walls and ceiling, only the golden sunflowers of the latter remaining, with the stained glass of the pulpit windows.

CAMPHILL QUEEN'S PARK CHURCH
Balvicar Drive

ADELAIDE PLACE BAPTIST CHURCH

188, Pitt Street

One of the few city centre churches still in active use. It was built in 1875–7 and designed by the versatile T L Watson. His Italian Renaissance building has some particularly fine features including the portico with double Corinthian columns. The interior is equally good.

An interesting and unusual Greek Revival building now secularised. It was designed by James Sellars, 'Greek' Thomson's most brilliant follower, and built in 1876—1878. The front has a fine Ionic portico surmounted by an attractive octagonal domed belfry while the sides are treated imaginatively with colonnaded windows. Hidden away in a side street, this fine building is not as well known as it deserves to be.

FINNIESTON FREE CHURCH

41, Derby Street

KELVINSIDE HILLHEAD PARISH CHURCH

Saltoun Street

The 13th century Sainte Chapelle in Paris has been the inspiration for many churches and this is a robust, Scottish example. The huge windows could have been the cause of instability in a neighbourhood honeycombed with coal pits, but they have been set in a solid framework more suitable both practically and visually, to the city environment. The massive turrets flanking the frontage illustrate this point. The necessary contrast is provided by the great wheel window and the more delicate angel figures.

The interior is astonishingly open and light for a Presbyterian kirk. There is only a small gallery for organ and choir at the back. Thus one has the full effect of the windows and their varied colours. James Sellars was the architect, and the date 1877—8.

CATHEDRAL SQUARE U P CHURCH

Cathedral Square

The congregation which built this spectacular church were among the narrowest of the 18th century sects which broke away from the Church of Scotland. However, ideas change, and when they were ousted from their old home by the North British Railway in 1878, they commissioned John Honeyman to design something very different from their old meeting-house. The result is the present ornate Italian Renaissance building.

By opening day — 30 May 1880, it had cost £20,000, including statues of Saints Peter and Paul and the four Evangelists as well as stained-glass windows. Quite a few eyebrows must have been raised at such extravagant innovations.

A church on a busy street which tends to pass unnoticed. Its solid dignity — true Scottish Revival — illustrates its architect's love of his country's mediaeval beauty. Simplicity, whether born of poverty or choice need be no bad thing. The solid massing and plain openings add up to a highly satisfying and picturesque composition. The architect was John A Campbell and the date 1888—9.

SHAWLANDS OLD PARISH CHURCH

1120, Pollokshaws Road

SAINT GEORGE'S IN THE FIELDS PARISH CHURCH

485, Saint George's Road

This splendid example of the late flowering of the Classical Revival in Glasgow designed by H and D Barclay in 1885 boasts many subtleties of design which mark it out from slavish copies of Greek temples. The Ionic portico with its fine sculpture of Christ feeding the multitude, by William Birnie Rhind, forms the outstanding feature.

The church was restored in 1972–3 but since closure in 1979 has been allowed to deteriorate. Further restoration work is now in progress.

This striking and unusual building was erected in 1886–7 as the Stockwell Free Church for a congregation moving out from the city centre. The architect, J B Wilson, chose modern Italian Renaissance as his style, a rare choice for the period when Gothic held sway. The richly decorated apse with its Corinthian columns and the tall campanile make an impressive contribution to the streetscape.

SAINT ALBERT'S CATHOLIC CHURCH
145, Albert Drive

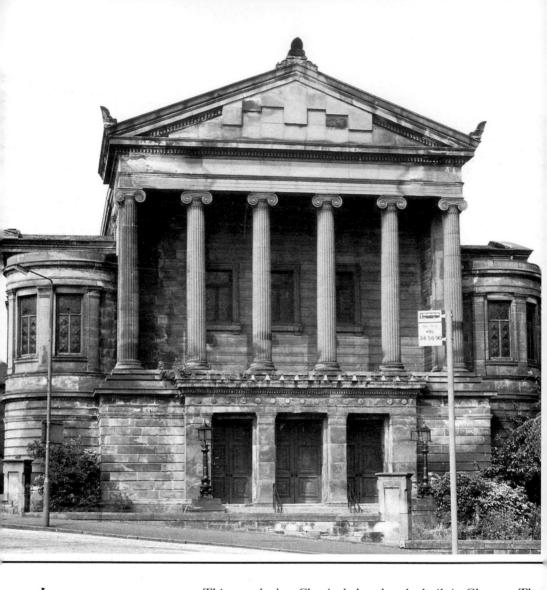

LANGSIDE FREE CHURCH
Battle Place

This was the last Classical church to be built in Glasgow. The plans were drawn up in 1894 and the Earl of Moray whose ancestors had fought Queen Mary at the Battle of Langside in 1568, laid the foundation-stone on 21 September 1895. Alexander Skirving, the architect, had been trained by 'Greek' Thomson, and the Greek Ionic portico is clearly a compliment to his great master. The style changes to Roman, however, at the sides. The incomplete tympanum of the pediment was intended to contain sculpture of John Knox exhorting the unhappy Queen Mary, with the Regent Moray looking on. The congregation decided not to spend the necessary £300 to have it carried out.

Since the church closed some years ago the interior has been vandalised. The latest proposal is to convert it into yet another licensed restaurant and club.

Having survived closure, motorway threats and vandalism, this building is now the headquarters of the Charles Rennie Mackintosh Society. They have lovingly repaired its broken windows and opened its doors as a permanent shrine to the great architect and designer.

The church was built in 1897—1899, at the same time as the first section of the School of Art, and is thus a product of that first maturity which saw some of his finest work. The perspective view is Mackintosh's own, showing the building in an idealised setting.

QUEEN'S CROSS CHURCH

866, Garscube Road

KELVIN STEVENSON MEMORIAL CHURCH
Belmont Street

With its crown steeple a familiar landmark high above the River Kelvin, this was originally the Nathaniel Stevenson Memorial Free Church, designed in 1898. The architect J J Stevenson was a relative.

The style is late Scottish Gothic owing something to both French Flamboyant and English Perpendicular. The open crown, that particularly Scottish feature, is modelled on that of King's College Chapel, Aberdeen. Just below are delightful carvings of birds and beasts — a squirrel eating nuts, two cocks ready for a fight, and a monkey, among others — a charming and thoroughly mediaeval touch.

EDUCATION

IRONWORK DETAIL
SCHOOL OF ART
167, RENFREW STREET

C R MACKINTOSH   ARCHITECT
1899

DUNDASVALE TEACHERS' CENTRE

6, New City Road

This building was the Normal School, and the first building in Britain to be erected specifically for the professional training of teachers. The mastermind behind the project was David Stow (1793—1864) the famous educationalist.

The architect was David Hamilton who provided a plain and functional building on three sides of a square, with ample space for recreation. It was opened on 31 October 1837 having cost £15,000, an enormous sum to be spent on education in those days.

This was erected in 1846–7 as Glasgow Academy, a private school for young gentlemen, designed by Charles Wilson. It is much better known as the High School of Glasgow which it became in 1878 when it was sold to the Glasgow School Board and the staff and pupils of the old Grammar School were transferred to it. Its Italian Renaissance front is enlivened by much fine sculpture including statues of Homer, Cicero, Galileo and James Watt. Local educational policy was responsible for the closure of the school in 1976, since when the buildings have been reconstructed for use by Strathclyde Regional Council.

STRATHCLYDE HOUSE

94, Elmbank Street

St Andrew's Catholic School

143, Greendyke Street

This attractive building now forms part of Our Lady and Saint Francis's School in Charlotte Street. It is little known, being tucked away in a corner of the street, and few people know of its existence.

It is one of the oldest educational buildings in the city having been built in 1855 and is unusually ornate for its date. The architect was probably Charles O'Neill.

Beside the modern college stands this unusual, impressive and neglected building. Built 1866—1868 as the Institution for the Deaf and Dumb, it was for many years the only establishment of its kind in Scotland.

The architect, James Ritchie of Salmon and Son, was greatly influenced by the contemporary English obsession with the Venetian Gothic style eulogized by John Ruskin. This is responsible also for its unusually colourful appearance due to the use of red and white stone. He seems to have pioneered polychromy in Glasgow.

The building became a College of Further Education in 1948 but has suffered increasing neglect after the erection of the new college in the 1960s. It deserves better treatment.

LANGSIDE COLLEGE ANNEXE

56, Prospecthill Road

The sham mediaevalism of Glasgow's Victorian University has become so familiar that it has won a sort of reluctant respect. For George Gilbert Scott, the London architect commissioned by the senate to design the buildings, the ideal was epitomised by the mediaeval quadrangles of Oxford and Cambridge. Edinburgh had seen its ideal in the Classicism of Robert Adam, and it would have seemed logical for the western metropolis to have chosen something more in keeping with its modern image. However 'Greek' Thomson was ignored (much to his disgust) and the opportunity lost.

Work began in 1866 with a vast workforce of 340 masons, 400 joiners, etc constructing the great complex of buildings. John Oldrid Scott, son of G G Scott designed the Bute Hall and substituted the present delicate spire for the original top-heavy one.

THE UNIVERSITY OF GLASGOW

University Avenue

ROCKVILLA SCHOOL

Dawson Road

When Glasgow School Board was set up in 1873 it found that education in the city was in a deplorable state, with about 35,000 children receiving no schooling of any kind. Plans for 16 new school buildings were prepared immediately and Rockvilla was one of those. Designed by John Honeyman, it had places for 889 pupils, and cost £6,000. The appearance is vaguely Tudor in style, with a circular tower housing the boys' staircase. Contemporary segregation demanded that the girls use a separate stair, divided from the boys' by a glass screen.

This school belongs to the second stage of building undertaken by the Glasgow School Board. Although the site had been purchased in 1874, it was not opened until 7 September 1877. The architect was John Burnet.

It was typical of its period although its vaguely mediaeval style was unusual. The tower with its slated spire is an attractive feature. Accommodation was provided for 983 children in classrooms seating various numbers from 48 to 130. The entrances and staircases, lined with sanitary white tiles, were specially praised. All in all it cost £10,000. In 1960 it became an Occupational Centre.

OVERNEWTON SCHOOL

52, Lumsden Street

KELVINSIDE ACADEMY

Bellshaugh Road

In June 1877 the Kelvinside Academy Company was formed to provide a private secondary school for Kelvinside and Hillhead. James Sellars was commissioned to design what was to be the finest school building in the city. At the time he was greatly influenced by the work of 'Greek' Thomson, and appropriately Greek was the ideal style for a school dedicated to Classical learning.

The opening took place on 2 September 1878, with an enrolment of 155, although places had been provided for 600. Happily there is no such problem in the 1980s.

Apart from the school building itself, Sellars designed scuplture, stained-glass, and much ironwork, which has been well looked-after and forms a most attractive feature.

BELLAHOUSTON ACADEMY

425, Paisley Road West

When compulsory education was introduced to Scotland in 1873 it applied to children of primary school age only. Secondary education was left in the hands of town councils and private bodies.

Bellahouston Academy was built to serve the Govan–Ibrox area and was opened on 26 August 1876. Its grand Franco-Scottish Gothic frontage, designed by Robert Baldie, is a prominent feature in Paisley Road West.

This building is of the greatest architectural and historical importance. It was the first of the Glasgow Board schools to be built on the central-hall plan, a revolutionary idea pioneered by the architects Hugh and David Barclay. Instead of rooms entering from a corridor, they are all reached from a central assembly hall with stairs and a balcony.

Abbotsford was the seventh school built on the south side to reduce the figure of 11,352 children who did not have a place in 1873. It was built to accommodate 1100 and was opened on 15 December 1879.

ABBOTSFORD PRIMARY SCHOOL
129, Abbotsford Place

DENNISTOUN PRIMARY SCHOOL

36, Meadowpark Street

Dennistoun began as a recognisable suburb about 1860 after a very slow start. Education was at first in the hands of private individuals but in 1881 Glasgow School Board decided that it was time for them to make a contribution. They chose a site at the east end, probably because that was convenient for the poorer parts. The architects — James Salmon and Son — designed a building in Tudor style capable of accommodating 1054 pupils. In 1895 an Infant School in Art Nouveau manner was built alongside.

Of all the School Boards set up in Scotland under the provisions of the 1872 Education Act, the Govan Parish Board was by far the most progressive. In 46 years they built 34 new schools and pioneered medical inspection, swimming baths, and education for the handicapped.

Govanhill was their 16th school, built in 1885−6 to serve the new burghs of Crosshill and Govanhill. The architects H and D Barclay designed a three storied Italian palazzo for 1010 pupils costing £8,911. It incorporates the typical Barclays' central hall.

GOVANHILL PRIMARY SCHOOL
27, Annette Street

GLASGOW SCHOOL OF ART

167, Renfrew Street

The history of this world-famous building is well known. The result of a competition held in 1896, it was designed by Charles Rennie Mackintosh and erected in two stages, not being completed until 1910. Fra Newbery, the director at the time, was the guiding hand behind the whole project and the result is as much a monument to him as it is to Mackintosh.

A plain building was asked for, and in some ways that is what they got, but the overall plainness is relieved by a variety and subtlety of ornament that entirely belies the first impression. The stark ultra-modern north front with its enormous studio windows is relieved by the use of (in the context) delicate ornamental ironwork.

The back is a complete contrast, and is in many ways more exciting than the front. Essentially Scottish even to the harling, it is a mighty mass built up of details from the great Baronial period of the 16th and 17th centuries to form a romantic skyline one does not expect in the centre of Glasgow.

The interior is full of interest both in the building itself with its magnificent use of timber, and in the collection of Mackintosh furniture.

COMMERCIAL

'MERCURY'
MERCANTILE CHAMBERS
53, BOTHWELL STREET

SALMON & GILLESPIE   ARCHITECTS
FRANCIS DERWENT WOOD AND JAMES YOUNG
SCULPTORS
1898

LANGSIDE HALL

5, Langside Avenue

Built in 1845−9, this ornate building was originally the National Bank, and stood at 57, Queen Street in the city centre. In the style of a Florentine palace, its facade is covered with carving. There are keystone heads over the lower openings representing the rivers Clyde, Thames, Shannon and Wye with the Royal Arms flanked by figures of Britannia and Plenty crowning the cornice. John Gibson of London was the architect and John Thomas the sculptor.

The building was moved stone by stone and reopened in its new role on 24 December 1903.

This superb example of a Roman palazzo was erected between 1854 and 1857 as the Glasgow head office of the Commercial Bank. The architect, David Rhind of Edinburgh, has employed a variety of stone facings to give that special feeling of strength and wealth. Sculpture plays a large part in the design with lots of nice lion heads, complacent at first glance, but quite capable, one feels of guarding the bank's treasures. Ornamental panels on the ground floor represent children stamping gold coins and printing banknotes — mid-Victorian humour which would not go down well today. The sculptor was Alexander Handyside Ritchie of Edinburgh.

THE ROYAL BANK OF SCOTLAND

8, Gordon Street

36,
JAMAICA
STREET

It was not until 1851 and the choice of the Crystal Palace to house the Great Exhibition in London that iron began to be taken seriously as a building material. Architects, however, remained sharply divided. In Glasgow the stylistic battles of the metropolis were heard only faintly. Cast-iron had long been in use here, and its combination with plate-glass an obvious development.

John Baird, an architect of wide experience, was able in this exceptional building to combine the Classical proportions of a Renaissance palace with the special qualities of a prefabricated structure. No one has done it better. Still in use as work and showrooms it has been maintained in excellent condition.

A building just opposite the main entrance to the Central Station and long known as the Grosvenor Building from its famous restaurant. The main four storey part of the present frontage is the office block built in 1864—5 and designed by Alexander and George Thomson. It illustrates many of the unique qualities of Alexander's design — closely-placed windows, pillars seemingly growing out of the wall, and a profusion of ornament. The unfortunate top storey was added in the early 1900s. The whole building has been reconstructed recently.

70—80, GORDON STREET

42, VIRGINIA STREET

Virginia Street — a name redolent of the time of the Tobacco Lords — has changed greatly since its elegant beginnings in the mid 18th century. It soon became commercialised, its houses turned into banks and offices. No 42 was built in 1866—1867 for the Glasgow Gas-light Company. It has a very bold frontage in Roman palace style, designed by R G Melvin. Recently the building was reconstructed as offices behind the original facade.

The most northerly of the group of buildings forming the west side of George Square, the Merchants' House follows the opulent Italian palazzo style of its predecessor on the south corner. Both frontages are marked by some fine sculpture. Particularly unusual are the reclining figures supporting the oriel windows. The original part of the building dates from 1874—7 and was designed by John Burnet. The sculptor was James Young.

THE MERCHANTS' HOUSE
7, West George Street

THE STOCK EXCHANGE

69, West George Street

A marvellous piece of Ruskinian Gothic placed right in the city centre where it acts as a splendid foil to the Renaissance of the surrounding buildings. Designed in 1874 the architect John Burnet purposely chose what he considered an appropriate style, and what could be more appropriate that that of the greatest of the mediaeval mercantile states?

The main Buchanan Street doorway has carved heads representing the races of the world — European, African, Indian and Chinese to maintain the trading association. With the exception of the two front walls the whole structure was rebuilt between 1969 and 1971.

Victorian banks liked to have impressive buildings to demonstrate their wealth and reliability. The Clydesdale was no exception and they held a competition in 1871 to choose an appropriately grand design for their new head-office. John Burnet was the winner with this opulent Venetian palace. As usual he made much use of sculpture to enrich the design, and this was executed by John Mossman.

The banking hall inside is also splendid, its coffered roof rising to an elliptical dome. The bank is to be congratulated on its recent work of restoration of this important building.

THE CLYDESDALE BANK

30, Saint Vincent Place

JAMES SELLARS HOUSE

144, West George Street

Built in 1877—1880 as the New Club, it was reconstructed behind the original facade in 1980—1981 and renamed James Sellars House after its illustrious architect.

The massive doorway is the most impressive part of the design. It contains some exquisite sculpture by William Mossman II.

An attractive and early example of the Franco-Flemish style in Glasgow. Designed in 1885 it was one of the first buildings in the city to be built of red sandstone — in this case from Ballochmyle in Ayrshire. Its delicate sculpture is also a feature. The building was erected for The Glasgow Evening Citizen, the pioneer $\frac{1}{2}$d newspaper in the United Kingdom. It is now occupied by a variety of offices.

24,
SAINT
VINCENT
PLACE

121, WEST GEORGE STREET

The 1890s saw a breakaway from the earlier favourite Classical and Italian Renaissance styles. They were replaced by what was considered the modern French style. One of the finest examples of this is the former Sun Fire and Life Insurance building of 1892–5. It is the only commercial building by its artist-architect William Leiper, and illustrates his care over details.

Sculpture plays an important part in the design and includes replicas of three Michaelangelo figures high on the west facade. The sculptor was William Birnie Rhind.

Mackintosh's own very personal perspective gives a far better idea of this building (formerly offices for the *Glasgow Herald*) than any photograph could do. It is an early work, being designed in 1893 at least partly in conjunction with John Keppie. The eye is drawn to the soaring octagonal corner tower with its ogival cap, which evidently owes something to the contemporary English Arts and Crafts movement.

60, MITCHELL STREET

THE
SAVOY CENTRE
140, Sauchiehall Street

Sauchiehall Street has seen many changes in the century and a half of its existence. From a farm road gradually lined with terraces and villas it has become a busy shopping precinct. This building, the second on the site, was built in 1892—3 as showrooms and warehouses for Messrs Cumming and Smith, a firm of house furnishers.

The frontage is a splendid affair showing the influence of the French Renaissance and 'Greek' Thomson. The architects were H and D Barclay. There is some very fine sculpture including 10 allegorical figures, by William Birnie Rhind.

This small but outstanding building stands at a busy corner in the city centre. Its very lack of size draws attention to it. In the modern French idiom, by John James Burnet who had been trained in Paris, it was designed in 1894. Its massive walls suggesting all the security of a vault, are offset by the beautiful sculpture. It was modelled by George Frampton and carved by William Shireffs.

TRUSTEE SAVINGS BANK
177, Ingram Street

THE CLYDESDALE BANK

91, Buchanan Street

This colourful architectural gem is set in a street of fine buildings. It was designed in 1895 as tea and luncheon rooms for the famous Miss Cranston, the architect being George Washington Browne. The red and cream stone came from Dumfriesshire and Newcastle respectively. Although the building was carefully restored recently, the fascinating interiors, by Mackintosh and George Walton, have long disappeared.

One of the most original buildings in the city centre, its tall, narrow idiosyncratic front, owing little to any historical style, immediately attracts attention. The ornamentation is quite unlike anything else in the city, and was the work of two important designers who were the real Art Nouveau architects of Glasgow, James Salmon II, and J Gaff Gillespie. Their work stands apart from both Mackintosh and the orthodox school, but like the former did not last. The date is 1899–1901.

144, SAINT VINCENT STREET

116,
HOPE STREET

No buildings express more clearly the commercial prosperity of the 1890s than those erected for the insurance companies. This typically exuberant German Renaissance frontage covered with carved ornamentation is only one of many in the city. It dates from 1899—1901 and was designed by the specialists in this particular field, J B and W A Thomson.

PUBLIC

LEGAL HEAD
PROCURATORS' LIBRARY
62, WEST GEORGE STREET

CHARLES WILSON   ARCHITECT
ALEXANDER HANDYSIDE RITCHIE   SCULPTOR
1856

147, BUCHANAN STREET

This building, the former Western Club, built in 1839–1842 to designs by David and James Hamilton, marked a significant development of the city's street architecture.

Barry had set the fashion in London for elaborate clubhouses designed as Italian palaces but this example is much more original in appearance.

Unfortunately the building was gutted and rebuilt in 1966 so that nothing remains of the fine interiors.

In 1841 a competition was held to provide new legal and administrative headquarters for the city. It was won by William Clarke and George Bell with this outstanding Greek Revival building now disused after the transfer of the Sheriff Court to new premises. The two contrasting porticoes illustrate the architects' imaginative use of an archaic style with skilful reuse for modern purposes. A new use must be found for this important early Victorian masterpiece.

40—50, WILSON STREET

THE PROCURATORS' HALL AND LIBRARY

62, West George Street

This is the headquarters of the legal profession in Glasgow. The architect, Charles Wilson, for obvious reasons, modelled his design on Sansovino's famous Library of Saint Mark in Venice.

The interior of the library on the upper floor is sumptuously treated with Corinthian pillars and elaborate plasterwork. The division of the area into alcoves for private study gives the whole concept a magical spatial quality.

OVERLEAF:

The exterior is richly ornamented with sculpture, and the lower windows each have a keystone carved with the head of a well-known legal figure of the time. Sculptor, Handyside Ritchie.

A striking frontage in what was considered in the 1850s the modern Franco-Italian style — effective, but not improved by being painted blue. A small theatre known as the *Britannia Music Hall* was constructed within the first and second floors of the building. In this century, under the ownership of A E Pickard, the name was changed to the *Panopticon*. The architects of the original building were Thomas Gildard and Robert H M Macfarlane.

109—115, TRONGATE

FIRST CHURCH OF CHRIST SCIENTIST

1, La Belle Place

This unusual and impressive building was erected in 1857–8 as the Queen's Rooms. Its originally fine interior has been gutted after a fire. The exterior, however, is largely unaltered, and the sculpture intact. The frieze is particularly fine illustrating the progress of civilisation and, on the north front, Minerva distributing gifts to representatives of the arts and sciences. Among the former is Charles Wilson, the architect, holding the plans. He is also commemorated, with the contractors, on the south gable of the building.

63

The Briggait

THE BRIGGAIT CENTRE

66, Clyde Street

This is the former Fish Market, designed by Clarke and Bell and opened on 8 December 1873. Two impressive French Renaissance facades conceal a high iron and glass roof, ideal for market purposes. The south front has some lively sculpture of winged sea-horses flanking medallions of an abnormally young Queen Victoria.

The Fish Market moved to new buildings in 1977 and after some years of indecision the old building has been reconstructed as a shopping centre for small retailers.

In England the Classical Revival faded before the united denunciation of Pugin and Ruskin, but in Glasgow those thunderings were but distantly heard. The example of 'Greek' Thomson was a more potent influence and Classicism persisted. James Sellars here, in the frontage of the old Saint Andrew's Halls managed to rival Thomson himself and to give the city one of its finest buildings. The sculpture — beautifully judged — is by John and William Mossman.

The interior was destroyed by fire in 1962 but has been rebuilt as the library extension with a small theatre.

MITCHELL LIBRARY EXTENSION
Granville Street

THE KIBBLE PALACE
THE BOTANIC GARDENS

Queen Margaret Drive

This well-known building began life as a conservatory at Coulport House on Loch Long in the 1860s. Various additions were made to it over the years and eventually in 1871 its owner John Kibble came to an arrangement with Glasgow Corporation by which it would be re-erected in the city as a concert hall. It seems that it was at that time that the central rotunda was added. For many years it was used for concerts and public meetings but in 1891 it was converted into a winter garden.

Private baths were popular with the middle-class Victorians. They were the recreation centres of their day and provided facilities for games and socializing.

The Turkish associations of bath-houses enabled architects to design suitably Eastern buildings with opulent brightly-coloured tiled interiors. The Western Baths were designed by Clarke and Bell and opened on 29 April 1878.

WESTERN BATHS

12, Cranworth Street

D. S. BADDELEY
ENGINEERING CO. LTD.

QUIPMENT

OX

19, MCALPINE STREET

John Carrick, the first City Architect, revolutionised the design of public buildings in Glasgow. He was one of the most influential figures of the Victorian era.

This building was originally the Marine Police Station, the tenth of the series of eleven new police buildings he designed between 1849 and 1890. In Italian Renaissance style it dates from 1882—4, and is one of only two which remain.

The City Hall built over the Bazaar or Fruit Market, was opened in 1841. There have been many changes since then. There have been new galleries and platform and reseating more than once. In 1885—6 the greatest drawback, the congested entrance to Albion Street was replaced by a new one at the other end of the building linked to a suite of rooms attached to the extended market. The fine Italian Renaissance frontage was designed by John Carrick.

THE CITY HALL

90, Candleriggs

THE VICTORIA INFIRMARY

Langside Road

Hospitals are essentially functional buildings and one does not expect very much in the way of architectural show in their design. Nevertheless, the Victorian architects made great efforts to provide their clients with buildings which combined the latest ideas in hygiene and patient-care with suitably impressive exteriors.

The Victoria Infirmary was designed in this way by James Sellars at the end of a brilliant career. The administrative block is particularly attractive with its fine carving and simple dignity. The architect did not live to see the opening in February 1890.

The highly desirable suburb of Pollokshields began in 1850 with some small cottages along the banks of the Paisley Canal. It was declared a Burgh in 1876 but it was not until 1890 that it had its own administrative buildings. They form a picturesque group on the edge of the Maxwell Park, and were designed by the Burgh architect H E Clifford who was also responsible for a number of the villas in the neighbourhood.

The hall is now administered by a charitable trust.

POLLOKSHIELDS BURGH HALL

72, Glencairn Drive

GOVAN BURGH HALL
401, Govan Road

Govan was probably the most successful of Glasgow's suburban burghs. It had grown from a small country village in the 1840s to one of the busiest industrial areas in a few decades. It contained two of the most important shipyards on the Clyde and its population soared. The original Burgh buildings of 1867–8 were soon too small and a competition in 1897 produced the grandiose complex seen here. The cost was £60,000 and the architects Thomson and Sandilands.

DOMESTIC

'TRIAL BY JURY' PANEL
40-50, WILSON STREET

CLARKE & BELL   ARCHITECTS
WALTER BUCHAN   SCULPTOR
1844

CLARENDON PLACE

Saint George's Cross

This is the small remaining fragment of what was originally intended to have been a grand new housing development on the lines of Waterloo Place at the east end of Princes Street, Edinburgh. Maryhill Road was to have been flanked by Corinthian porticoes and terraces leading up to a grand circus. As so often the finances could not keep up with the grandiose design and it came to premature halt. This corner block has recently been restored. Alexander Taylor, architect 1839—41.

The Italian Palazzo was the model for so many Glasgow buildings that one tends to forget its origin in the sunny south. It was an easy style to adapt for many different requirements — office-blocks, terraces, or even the familiar tenements. Wherever a three or four storey building was required architects immediately thought of the streets of Rome, Florence or the canals of Venice. Garnethill has a number of good examples of different types. This block was built in 1841–2.

PEEL TERRACE
104–110, Hill Street

CLAREMONT TERRACE

Glasgow's spread westward in the early years of Victoria's reign was marked by the building of many fine, restrained Renaissance terraces. Among the most attractive developments are those climbing Woodlands Hill from Charing Cross to Park Circus. The beauty of the buildings is enhanced by their setting amongst private gardens, Edinburgh style.

Claremont Terrace was built between 1842 and 1850, John Baird I being the architect. Really a crescent, the frontage is enlivened with Greek Ionic porches and delicate wrought-iron balconies.

The Great Western Road is undoubtedly the finest approach to the city and it is appropriate that some of the most splendid buildings should be found along its route. Kirklee (originally Windsor) Terrace was the earliest of the buildings on the Kelvinside estate and set a standard of excellence for the whole development. Charles Wilson was the architect and he chose Florentine Renaissance as his style. Although started in 1845 the terrace took twenty years to complete.

KIRKLEE TERRACE

Great Western Road

SAINT VINCENT CRESCENT

The Stobcross estate was sold in 1844 and the northern half laid out as a spectacular housing development four years later. The architect was Alexander Kirkland, and he took as his model the mid 18th century developments in Bath.

The Stobcross plan was that of a huge ellipse with a central garden, and two streets leading off it. The eastern entrance was marked by boldly curved corners. Much has been done recently to renovate this important example of Victorian planning.

Built in 1855—1858 this has recently become the most famous of the Kelvinside Terraces due to its spectacular reconstruction after a disastrous fire in 1978 which destroyed its eastern half. It was described in 1858 as 'the finest Range of Buildings in Great Britain, being designed after the most palatial style of architecture . . .' The architect, J T Rochead, designed the whole terrace in identical units of five bays which could have been repeated endlessly one feels into the western sunset.

GROSVENOR TERRACE
Great Western Road

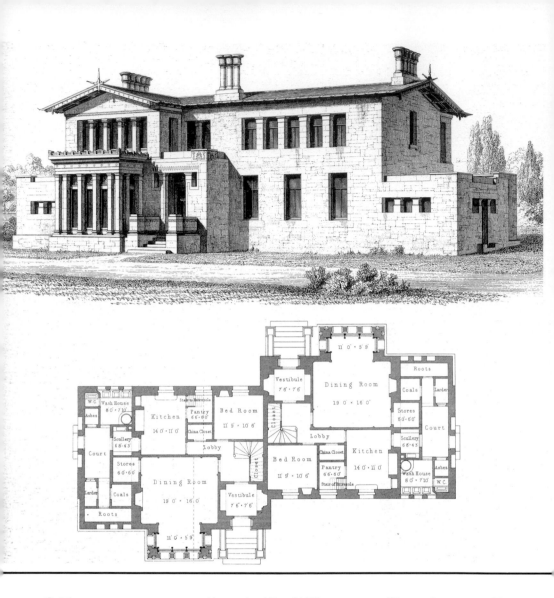

25, MANSIONHOUSE ROAD

Alexander 'Greek' Thomson was Glasgow's supreme Victorian architect. He had all the qualities of a great designer, ingenuity in planning, an innate sense of the rightness of things, and a passion for detail. This double villa in Langside was built in 1857 and illustrates all these characteristics.

The plan is ingenious with the houses facing in opposite directions allowing for greater variety of treatment of elevation than would otherwise have been possible. Large windows, often in colonnades, chimney-cans designed as lotus flowers, and all the other features, add up to a building of outstanding originality and importance.

The development of the Park area in the 1850s by Glasgow Corporation is now recognised as one of the most spectacular civic planning schemes in Britain. In its own way it echoes Bath although a century later, and Charles Wilson obviously tried to reproduce the grandeur and excitement of the English city here on a Glasgow hilltop.

The buildings, both Italian and French in inspiration have a marvellous setting above the park, and with their elaborate interiors formed fitting homes for the first generation of Victorian merchants and industrialists.

PARK TERRACE

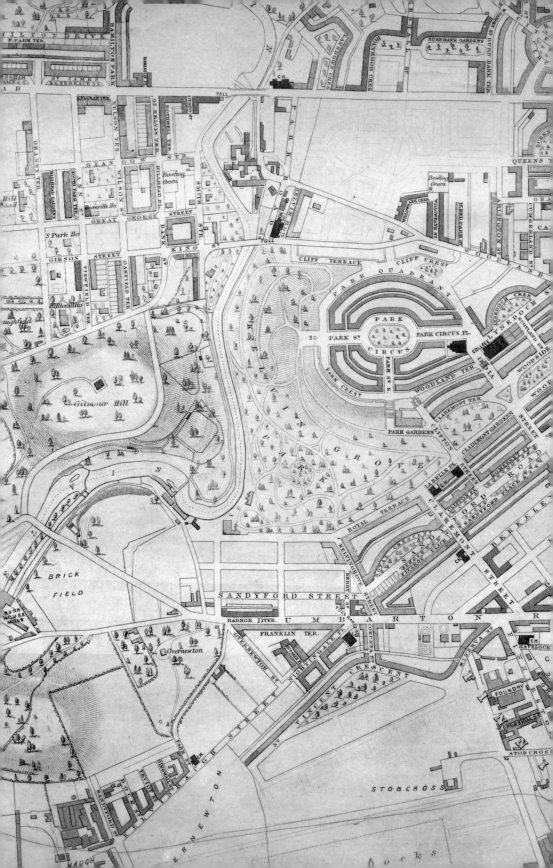

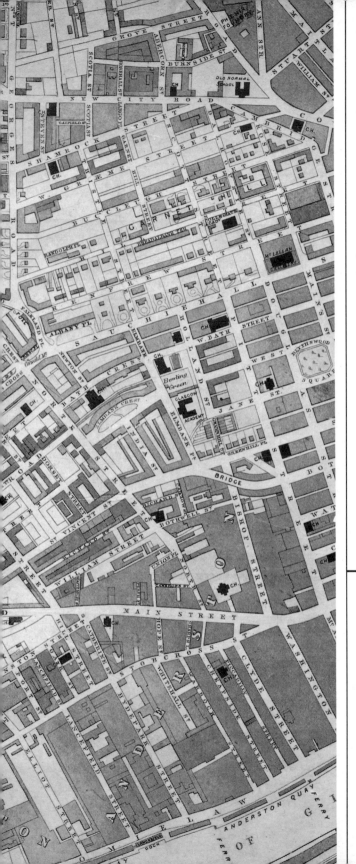

THE
PARK AREA
1866

WALMER CRESCENT

Paisley Road West

This is 'Greek' Thomson the monumental designer. For boldness and originality it takes some beating. He has purposely avoided almost all ornament relying for effect on uncompromising simplicity and massing. The bow windows are uniquely treated, four being joined together to form striking rectangular projections from the face of the building. The continuous colonnade of the top floor serves to give maximum lighting and also to unify the facade. An unqualified masterpiece.

The earliest part of the BBC's complex is the Renaissance palace built in 1869–1871 for John Bell. He was the wealthy and cultured owner of the Glasgow Pottery at Port Dundas, the largest pottery in Scotland.

    He wanted his house to show his impeccable architectural taste and also to contain a gallery for the exhibition of his large collection of paintings. These wishes were splendidly fulfilled by his architect J T Rochead at a cost of £50,000. It has been the property of the BBC since 1938.

BROADCASTING HOUSE
Queen Margaret Drive

998, GREAT WESTERN ROAD

The Kelvinside estate was planned as early as 1839 when a layout by the London architect Decimus Burton was proposed. It was too far out of town, however, and feuing was very slow. After 30 years only 50 plots had been built on and they were for terrace houses. It was not until 1869 that the first villa was built.

In 1873 eleven acres on the north side of Great Western Road were bought by Thomas Russell of the Saracen Foundry for development. Villas costing not less than £2,000 were to be erected, plans being provided by James Boucher. This impressive Italian palace was built in 1877 for James Marshall, another partner in the Foundry. It boasts one of the most ornate interiors in the city, and is now owned by a private club.

The most ambitious range of tenements in central Glasgow. They were erected in 1889—1891, and were designed by J J Burnet and John A Campbell. The cost was £20,000. The elaborate French Renaissance frontage with its oriels, steep roofs and sumptuous carving, provides one of the most exciting pieces of streetscape in the city. The choice of red stone — the first time it was used for a building of this size — must have greatly increased the impact of this striking frontage. The sculptor was William Birnie Rhind.

CHARING CROSS MANSIONS

Sauchiehall Street &
Saint George's Road

733–745, TERREGLES AVENUE

By the 1890s tenement design had reached a high degree of sophistication as can be seen by varying types all over the city. H E Clifford designed this range of six tenements in an attractive restrained style for Alexander Muir and Sons, builders, in 1895–6. He preferred, wherever possible, to use a white stone, even after the almost complete change-over to red around 1890.

One of the later houses to be built on the Kelvinside estate, Stoneleigh dates from 1900—1901, and was designed by H E Clifford. He was one of the most distinguished city architects of the time and specialised in domestic work.

His favourite style was English Tudor and this example is one of the best. It has all the elements of picturesque composition — a solid crenellated tower and a lower house with porch, large bow windows, balustraded terrace etc. The house was converted to a home for the elderly in the 1950s.

STONELEIGH
48, Cleveden Drive

SUNLIGHT COTTAGES

Kelvingrove Park

A little bit of old England in the heart of Glasgow. This picturesque group of cottages is the last remnant of the 1901 International Exhibition to remain in situ. It is a reproduction of housing built for Lever Brothers at Port Sunlight in Cheshire and was designed by James Miller the Exhibition's chief architect.

MISCELLANEOUS

PANEL WELLINGTON MEMORIAL
QUEEN STREET

CARLO MAROCHETTI SCULPTOR
1844

WELLINGTON MEMORIAL

Queen Street

Few celebrities see monuments erected in their honour during their lifetime, and the Duke of Wellington is not the obvious candidate. After the popularity won at Waterloo in 1815 he turned to politics where his opposition to reform soon drastically changed public opinion. In 1840 it was decided to erect an equestrian monument and Carlo Marochetti was chosen as sculptor. Completed in 1844, the bronze figure and its four panels with their rather peculiar Scottish flavour, are probably his finest work.

Initiative and imagination are not qualities much in evidence on the Clyde these days. One has only to look at the river and the streets around it to become utterly disillusioned. Compare this with what is happening to similar areas in London and Liverpool where the old docks are being given a new lease of life.

Could anything be more depressing than these splendid Classical warehouses dating from the 1850s and 1860s mouldering uselessly away? The Clyde made Glasgow the second city of the Empire — surely it deserves better treatment than this? Happily improvement plans are now in hand.

44—54, JAMES WATT STREET

THE
NECROPOLIS
Cathedral Square

THE
MONTEATH
MAUSOLEUM

David Cousin, architect   *1842—3*

Occupying the rocky height overlooking the mediaeval
cathedral, the Necropolis is one of the world's most romantic
cemeteries. Planned in 1831 and opened two years later it
quickly became the most popular place of sepulture. At that time
the garden cemetery was a novel idea but it proved a most
pleasant alternative to the small overcrowded burial grounds in
the city centre.

   The setting lent itself to further adornment with splendid
architectural monuments and some of them are shown here.

94

JOHN HENRY ALEXANDER MONUMENT

James Hamilton II, architect   1852—3
A Handyside Ritchie, sculptor

95

CHARLES
TENNANT OF
SAINT ROLLOX
MONUMENT

Patric Park, sculptor   1839

THE AIKEN
OF DALMOAK
MAUSOLEUM

James Hamilton II,
architect   1875

SOUTHERN NECROPOLIS LODGE

316, Caledonia Road

The Southern Necropolis was proposed in 1840 to replace the overcrowded Gorbals Burial Ground, and to serve the south side of the city. A garden cemetery like the Necropolis, it lacks the romantic setting of its predecessor.

Charles Wilson designed the ornamental gateway in 1848. It takes the form of a Romanesque tower with an oriel window which gives a view of the whole cemetery.

Not many people know that there are two suspension bridges in the city. The well-known one from Clyde Street to Carlton Place was built in 1851 and reconstructed 20 years later. Saint Andrew's is in the east end and links Bridgeton and Hutchesontown. It has a 220 ft span with Classical pylons at each end. It comes as a surprise to find that the Roman Corinthian columns are made of cast-iron.

The architect was Charles O'Neil and the engineer Neil Robson. The Lord Provost opened the bridge on 23 August 1855 and thereafter one had to pay 2d per week for the privilege of using it.

SAINT ANDREW'S SUSPENSION BRIDGE

McNeil Street

60,
BODEN STREET

Glasgow once had many potteries, the earliest using the indigenous clay in the east end of the city. Later, with the production of finer wares the locations changed to cut the cost of transport.

Very little now remains of the pottery buildings. This range of brick warehouses formed part of Frederic Grosvenor's Bridgeton or Eagle Pottery built in 1869, famous for its salt glaze jars.

A striking building in the heart of that part of the east end known as 'Barrowland'. It formed the main part of William White & Son's clay-pipe factory which in their heyday produced 14,400 pipes per day in about 700 designs. Matthew Forsyth's frontage was originally intended to be in stone but costs dictated its construction in brick instead. It dates from 1876—7.

42, BAIN STREET

QUEEN STREET
STATION

The Edinburgh and Glasgow Railway Company opened their line on 18 February 1842 having blasted a tunnel of nearly $\frac{3}{4}$ of a mile to bring their terminus into the city centre. The station we see today with its splendid iron and glass vault was designed by the North British Railway's chief engineer James Carswell, and built 1878—1880. It is the only one of its kind in Scotland.

John Stewart Templeton commissioned William Leiper to design a splendid ornamental frontage towards the Green when extending his carpet factory in 1888. The architect decided to base his design very loosely on the Doge's palace at Venice. The walls are of bright red brick with coloured glazed bricks and glittering blue mosaic. The building as we see it today is a rebuilding of 1890, the original having collapsed with considerable loss of life in November 1889.

TEMPLETON'S BUSINESS CENTRE
Glasgow Green

103

SUNDIAL

The King's Park

This ornate obelisk dial was made in 1885 for the Earl of Hume and originally stood in the garden of Douglas Castle. It is in fact a copy of a dial erected at Newbattle Abbey, Midlothian, in 1635. The actual dials are on an octagonal stage supported by four caryatids and there are grotesque heads above. The sundial was re-erected in the King's Park at the entrance to the walled garden in 1958.

This elaborate monument, spectacular even in ruin, was Doulton and Company's chief exhibit at the 1888 Exhibition. Presented to the city afterwards, it was removed to Glasgow Green in 1890.

Recently the beautiful terracotta figures have been seriously vandalised and the whole fountain epitomizes a city in decay. Restoration is long overdue.

THE DOULTON FOUNTAIN
Glasgow Green

GOVAN SHIPBUILDERS OFFICES

1048, Govan Road

Few shipyards can boast a range of offices as fine as these but, of course, few shipyards have been as important as Fairfield's. John Elder began shipbuilding on this site in 1863 and so quickly did the firm expand that by the 1880s under the direction of Sir William Pearce and his son, it became the foremost yard on the Clyde.

John Keppie designed the long range of offices in French Renaissance style in 1889—1890 and is one of his most satisfactory works.

Cessnock or Prince's Dock was the third of the big docks on the River Clyde to be constructed in the heyday of the city's importance as a centre for mercantile shipping. It was opened on 10 September 1897.

Its 35 acres have been filled in during the 1980s and the Garden Festival of 1988 occupies its site.

The hydraulic pumping station which operated the cranes was the dock's only architectural feature and it has been preserved. Designed by J J Burnet and John A Campbell in 1894 it has a massive tower at one end, and an octagonal chimney inspired by the Tower of the Winds in Athens at the other.

PRINCE'S DOCK PUMPING STATION

Govan Road

THE TRAVEL CENTRE

Saint Enoch Square

Originally the ticket-office of Saint Enoch Underground Station, this delightful little building has now been adapted as a travel office. The Underground Railway was constructed 1890—1896 but, unlike the Central Low-level line, did not have many surface buildings. Because of its isolated and important position, considerable thought was given to the design of this one. James Miller, the foremost railway architect of the time, in Glasgow, designed the small-scale building in Jacobean style.

INDEX

Abbotsford Place   31
Abbotsford Place Primary School   31
Aberdeen King's College Chapel   18
Adam Robert   1728-1792   architect   25
Adelaide Place Baptist Church   8
Aiken of Dalmoak Mausoleum, Necropolis   97
Albert Drive, Pollokshields   15
Albion Street   69
Alexander John Henry   1796-1851   actor manager   95
Annette Street, Govanhill   33
Art Nouveau   53
Athens   107

Bain Street   101
Baird John (I)   1798-1859   architect   40 76
Baldie Robert   died 1890   architect   30
Ballochmyle stone   47
Balvicar Drive   7
Barclay Hugh & David   architects   14 31 33 50
Barrowland   101
Barry Sir Charles   1795-1860   architect   56
Bath Street   78
Battle of Langside   16
Battle Place   16
Bazaar   69
Bell George (I)   c1811-1887   architect   57 64 67 73
Bell John   1806-1880   potter   85
Bellahouston Academy   30
Bellshaugh Road   28
Belmont Street   18
Boden Street   100
Bothwell Street   37
Boucher James   died 1906   architect   86
Bridgeton   99

Bridgeton or Eagle Pottery   100
Briggait Centre   64
Britannia Music Hall   61
BBC Broadcasting House   85
Brown James   c1813-1878   architect   frontispiece
Browne Sir George Washington   1853-1939
    architect   52
Buchan Walter   died 1878   sculptor   73
Buchanan of Dowanhill Monument,
    Necropolis   frontispiece
Buchanan Street   44 52 56
Burnet John   1814-1901   architect   4 27 43 44 45
Burnet Sir John James   1857-1938
    architect   51 87 107
Burton Decimus   1800-1881   architect   86

Caledonia Road   2 98
Caledonia Road U P Church   2
Campbell John Archibald   1860-1909
    architect   13 87 107
Camphill Queen's Park Church   7
Candleriggs   69
Carlton Place   99
Carrick John   1819-1890   architect   68 69
Carswell James   c1833-1897   civil engineer   102
Cast iron   40 66 99
Cathedral Square   12
Cathedral Square U P Church   12
Cessnock or Prince's Dock   107
Charing Cross   76 87
Charing Cross Mansions   87
Christ Scientist First Church of   62
City Hall   69
Claremont Terrace   76
Clarendon Place   74
Clarke & Bell   architects   57 64 67 73
Clarke William   1809-1889   architect   57 64 67 73
Cleveden Drive   89
Clifford Henry Edward   1852-1932
    architect   71 88 89
Clyde River   72 93 107
Clyde Street   64 99

Clydesdale Bank   45   52
Commercial Bank   39
Coulport House, Loch Long   66
Cousin David   1809-1878   architect   94
Cranston Catherine   1849-1934   restaurateur   52
Cranworth Street   67
Crosshill Burgh   33
Crystal Palace, London   40
Cumming & Smith   house furnishers   50

Dawson Road   26
Deaf and Dumb Institution (former)   23
Dennistoun Primary School   32
Derby Street   9
Doge's Palace, Venice   103
Douglas Castle   104
Doulton & Company   terra cotta manufacturers   105
Doulton Fountain   105
Dundasvale Teachers' Centre   20

Eagle Pottery   100
Edinburgh & Glasgow Railway Company   102
Edinburgh University   25
Elder John   1824-1869   shipbuilder   106
Elgin Place Congregational Church (former)   4
Elmbank Street   21
Exhibition Great, London 1851   40
Exhibition International 1888   105
Exhibition International 1901   90

Fairfield Shipyard, Govan   106
Finnieston Free Church   9
First Church of Christ Scientist   62
Fish Market (former)   64
'The Follies'   4
Forsyth Matthew   1850-1880   architect   101
Frampton Sir George James   1860-1928   sculptor   51
Free Church College   3
Free College Church   3
Fruit Market (former)   69

Garden Festival 1988   107
Garnethill   *ix* 75
Garscube Road   17
George Square   43
Gibson John   1819-1892   architect   38
Gildard Thomas   1822-1895   architect   61
Gillespie John Gaff   1870-1926   architect   37 53
Glasgow Academy (first)   21
Glasgow Evening Citizen   47
Glasgow Gas-light Company   42
Glasgow Green   103 105
Glasgow Herald   49
Glasgow Pottery   85 100
Glasgow School Board   26 27 31 32
Glasgow School of Art   17 19 34 35 36
Glasgow University   25
Glencairn Drive, Pollokshields   71
Gorbals Burial Ground   98
Gordon Street   39 41
Govan Burgh Hall   72
Govan Parish School Board   33
Govan Road   72 106 107
Govan Shipbuilders   106
Govanhill Burgh   33
Govanhill Primary School   33
Grammar School, Old   21
Granville Street   65
Great Western Road   6 77 79 86
Greendyke Street   22
Grosvenor Building   41
Grosvenor Frederic   died 1915   potter   100
Grosvenor Terrace   79

Hamilton David   1768-1843   architect   20 56
Hamilton James (I)   died 1861   architect   56
Hamilton James (II)   died 1894   architect   95 97
High School (former)   21
Hill Street, Garnethill   75
Honeyman John   1831-1914   architect   6 12 26
Hope Street   54
Hughes Henry   1822-1883   stained-glass artist   6
Hutchesontown   99

Ingram Street   51
Institution for the Deaf and Dumb (former)   23
Ironwork   19   29

Jamaica Street   40
James Watt Street   93
'John Street Jam'   5
John Street U P Church   5

Kelvin River   18
Kelvin Stevenson Memorial Church   18
Kelvingrove Park   90
Kelvinside Academy   28   29
Kelvinside Estate   77   79   86   89
Kelvinside Hillhead Parish Church   10
Keppie John   1862-1945   architect   49   106
Kibble John   engineer   66
Kibble Palace   66
King's College Chapel, Aberdeen   18
King's Park, The   104
Kirkland Alexander   c1823-1892   architect   78
Kirklee Terrace   77
Knox John   reformer   16

La Belle Place   62
Langside   80
Langside Avenue   38
Langside Battle of, 13 May 1568   16
Langside College   23
Langside Free Church   16
Langside Hall   38
Langside Road   70
Lansdowne Church   6
Leiper William   1839-1916   architect   7   48   103
Lever Brothers   90
Library Mitchell   65
Library of Saint Mark, Venice   58
Library Procurators'   55   58   59   60
Low-level Railway   108
Lumsden Street   27
Lynedoch Street   5

McAlpine Street   68
Macfarlane Robert H M   died 1862   architect   61
Mackintosh Charles Rennie   1868-1928
   architect   17   19   34   35   36   49   52   53
Mackintosh Charles Rennie, Society   17
NcNeil Street   99
Mansionhouse Road, Langside   80
Marine Police Station (former)   68
Marochetti Baron Carlo   1805-1867   sculptor   91   92
Marshall James   ironfounder   86
Mary Queen of Scots   16
Maryhill Road   74
Maxwell Park   71
Meadowpark Street, Dennistoun   32
Melvin Robert Grieve   architect   42
Mercantile Chambers, Bothwell Street   37
Merchants' House   43
Michaelangelo Buonarroti   1475-1563   sculptor   48
Miller James   1860-1947   architect   90   108
Mitchell Library   65
Mitchell Street   49
Monteath Mausoleum, Necropolis   94
Mossman John   1817-1890   sculptor   7   45   65
Mossman William (II)   1824-1884   sculptor   6   46   65
Muir Alexander & Sons   builders   88

National Bank, Queen Street   38
Necropolis   94   95   96   97   98   frontispiece
New City Road   20
New Club (former)   46
Newbattle Abbey, Midlothian   104
Newbery Francis   1855-1946   artist   34
Normal School (former)   20
North British Railway   12   102
North Park House   85

O'Neill Charles   architect   22   29
Our Lady and Saint Francis Catholic School   22
Overnewton School   27

Paisley Canal   71
Paisley Road West   30   84

'Panopticon The'   61
Park area   81 82 83
Park Patric   c1810-1855   sculptor   96
Park Terrace   81
Pearce Sir William   c1833-1888   shipbuilder   106
Peel Terrace, Hill Street   75
Pickard Albert Ernest   1875-1964
   cinema proprietor   61
Pitt Street   8
Pollokshaws Road   13
Pollokshields   71
Pollokshields Burgh Hall   71
Port Dundas   *ix* 85
Port Sunlight, Cheshire   90
Prince's Dock (former)   107
Procurators' Library   55 58 59 60
Prospecthill Road   23
Pugin Augustus Welby Northmore   1812-1852
   architect   65

Queen Margaret Drive   66 85
Queen Street   92
Queen Street Station   102
Queen Victoria   1819-1901   *ix* 64
Queen's Cross Church   17
Queen's Rooms   62

Renfrew Street   19 34 35 36
Rhind David   1801-1883   architect   39
Rhind William Birnie   1853-1933
   sculptor   14 48 50 87
Ritchie Alexander Handyside   1804-1870
   sculptor   39 55 59 95
Ritchie James   1835-1910   architect   23
Robson Neil   1808-1869   civil engineer   99
Rochead John Thomas   1814-1878
   architect   5 79 85
Rockvilla School   26
Rowan William Gardner   1845-1924   1
Royal Bank of Scotland   39
Ruskin John   1819-1900   art critic   23 44 65
Russell Thomas   ironfounder   86

Saint Albert's Catholic Church   15
Saint Andrew's Catholic School   22
Saint Andrew's Halls (former)   65
Saint Andrew's Suspension Bridge   99
Saint Enoch Square   108
Saint Enoch Subway Station   108
Saint George's Cross   74
Saint George's in the Fields Church   14
Saint George's Road   14   87
Saint Vincent Crescent   78
Saint Vincent Place   45   47
Saint Vincent Street   53
Sainte Chapelle, Paris   10
Salmon and Son   architects   23   32
Salmon James (II)   1873-1924   architect   37   53
Saltoun Street   10   11
Sansovino Jacopo   1486-1570   architect   58
Saracen Foundry   86
Sauchiehall Street   50
Savoy Centre   50
School of Art   17   34   35   36
Scott John Oldrid   1841-1913   architect   25
Scott Sir George Gilbert   1810-1877
   architect   25
Sculpture   1   6   7   14   18   37   38   39   43   44   45
   46   48   50   51   55   59   62   64   65   70   87   91   94
   95   97
Sellars James   1843-1888   architect   9   10   11   28
   29   46   65   70
Sellars House, James   46
Shanks James   died 1864   sculptor   6
Shawlands Old Parish Church   13
Sheriff Court (former)   57
Shireffs William   died 1902   sculptor   51
Skirving Alexander   died 1919   architect   16
Southern Necropolis   98
Stained glass   6   7   11
Statues   12   21   37   65   96
Stevenson John James   1831-1908   architect   18
Stevenson Memorial Church   18
Stobcross Estate   78
Stock Exchange   44

Stockwell Free Church (former)   15
Stoneleigh, Cleveden Drive   89
Stow David   1793-1864   educationalist   20
Strathbungo Parish Church (former)   1
Strathclyde House   21
Strathclyde Regional Council   21
Subway   108
Sun Fire & Life Insurance Company   48
Sundial   104
Sunlight Cottages, Kelvingrove Park   90
Suspension bridges   99

Taylor Alexander   died 1846   architect   74
Templeton John Stewart   died 1918
    carpet manufacturer   103
Templeton's Business Centre   103
Tennant Charles of Saint Rollox   1768-1838   96
Terregles Avenue, Pollokshields   88
Thomas John   1813-1862   sculptor   38
Thomson Alexander 'Greek'   1817-1875
    architect   2   4   9   16   25   28   41   65   80   84
Thomson Alexander & George   architects   41
Thomson & Sandilands   architects   72
Thomson James Baird   died 1917   architect   54
Thomson William Aitken   died 1947   architect   54
Tobacco Lords   42
Tower of the Winds, Athens   107
Travel Centre   108
Trinity House   3
Trongate   61

Underground Railway   108
University Avenue   25
University of Glasgow   25

Venice, Doge's Palace   103
Venice, Saint Mark's Library   58
Victoria Infirmary   70
Virginia Street   42

Walmer Crescent   84
Walton George   1867-1933   designer   52
Waterloo Place, Edinburgh   74
Watson Thomas Lennox   1850-1920   architect   8   47
Webster Alfred A   died 1915   stained-glass artist   6
Wellington Memorial   91 92
West George Street   43 44 46 48 55 58 59 60
Western Baths   67
Western Club (former)   56
White & Son, William   clay-pipe manufacturers   101
Wilson Charles   1810-1863   architect   3   21   55   58
     59   60   62   77   81   98
Wilson John Bennie   c1848-1923   architect   15
Wilson Street   57   73
Wood Francis Derwent   1871-1926   sculptor   37
Woodlands Estate   76

Young James   sculptor   37   43